The Color Nature Library
AQUARIUM FISHES

By
JANE BURTON

Designed by
DAVID GIBBON

Produced by
TED SMART

CRESCENT BOOKS

3

INTRODUCTION

Fishes are among the most miraculously beautiful of animals, exquisite in colour, diverse in shape and form, lively and graceful in movement and fascinating in their behaviour. Many centuries ago now, in ancient China, men first took fishes from the lake or pond and kept them in special earthenware bowls, the better to observe and appreciate them. From such simple beginnings the art of fish-keeping spread until today it is one of the world's most popular hobbies.

I first started keeping fishes when I was about nine years old, beginning with the same species, probably, as was first kept by the ancient Chinese: the Goldfish. Like them, I took my fish from a pond and kept them in large bowls, but in my case the Goldfish were caught by the jam jar method in the ornamental ponds of the nearby town's municipal gardens, and the bowls I kept them in were not elegant earthenware but utility enamel. I caught black goldfish and orange ones. Boys said the black were poisonous like toads; my parents made me put them all back anyway, black or golden, because they were stolen. So my earliest venture into fish-keeping came to an abrupt end.

Next I began bringing home Three-spined Sticklebacks from the stream, and these I was encouraged to keep in large glass accumulator jars or small aquarium tanks whose puttied seams were always springing leaks. My observations of these sticklebacks made me think then that they had a sense of humour. One resplendent red-throated male built a nest in a long narrow tank and raised a young family. I released him, his two wives and his tiny brood back into the stream when the young were quite well grown; they were probably soon eaten by all the natural predators among which I unwarily dumped them, but it made me very happy at the time to let them go. It must have been beginner's luck to hatch and rear stickles in such a tank, for since then I have not always managed to get them to breed just when I want them to. I have also had to modify my ideas on the sense of humour of sticklebacks, since experience has proved them to be the most dour and sobersided amongst a whole order of sobersides. They are not even credited with an ability to play. The only fishes acknowledged to show any playful tendencies are members of the family that contains the Elephant-trunk Fish, a species I did not meet until twenty years later. This quaint small black fish from the rivers of West Africa has a brain-to-body ratio comparable to our own and will sometimes play for hours on end with a leaf, a ball of tinfoil or some other small toy.

A part of the interest I discovered in keeping sticklebacks was in reconstructing in miniature the natural habitat from which they came. I brought home stones, gravel, water plants and even other inhabitants of the stream such as caddis grubs and small water beetles. I also collected all sorts of live food to feed them on: mosquito larvae from the rain-water butts, daphnia from a static water tank, tiny invertebrates from the stickles' own stream. This no doubt accounts in large measure for the success I had in breeding them, for the fishes felt at home and were fed on natural foods.

All fish, whether such humble 'tiddlers' or the most delicate exotics, fare best if the tank in which they are kept approximates as nearly as possible to the environment from which they have been taken. The setting up and main-tenance of an aquarium in which any given fish species will be most at home requires much research and a sensitivity to that fish's needs.

There are many small tropical species that appear to thrive in mixed company, in a brightly-lit tank, planted with a variety of decorative plants. They give a great deal of pleasure to their owners, who can enjoy watching their glowing colours and lively movements. But of greater interest is the tank that in itself might not appeal so much to the eye but probably contains happier fishes. This tank is to the purely decorative one as a piece of jungle is to the formal garden. It contains not only growing plants but jumbled rocks and roots for the fishes to hide among. The water may not be crystal-clear but tea-coloured and peaty, if that is what the species prefers. The tank may be only dimly lit, or contain no plants at all; but where a particular species' needs are catered for it will feel at home and behave naturally. Under these conditions fishes will grow and flourish, assume their full beauty of coloration and reward their keeper with the spectacle of their courtship rituals and family life. This opportunity of observing the natural behaviour of fishes is one of the most rewarding aspects of aquarium keeping.

Left The Mandarin-fish displays its colourful dorsal fin
as it hovers in midwater above corals.

Pages 2-3 A pair of Discus, elegant but nervous creatures,
thrive only in soft peaty water among thick clumps of
Amazon plants.

Shoalers

Some of the most beautiful small fishes available to the aquarist are also some of the hardiest. The Guppy *top right* is the most popular of all aquarium fishes, being exceptionally robust and prolific under all sorts of conditions. A large number of beautifully coloured forms have been bred with large flowing fins or lyre-shaped or pointed tails. Also exceptionally easy to keep and breed is the Three-spot Gourami *top left*. A small shoal will flourish in a brightly-lit well planted tank, and this species is not at all fussy in its choice of foods. Neon Tetras *bottom left* look stunning when their iridescent stripes glow against a black background. In the wild they inhabit dark forest pools, but in the aquarium are not fastidious and thrive in all kinds of conditions, although they are not easy to breed. Rosy Tetras are also easy to keep but difficult to breed. Several species are imported. Largest of the group is the Bleeding Heart Tetra with the blood-red spot on its flank; three young ones are shoaling happily with two Rosies *bottom right*.

Surface Feeders

In the wild, a number of fish species co-exist because some live close to the surface, some feed in mid water, while others grub about the bottom. In the aquarium, also, species live at their own levels. Among surface dwellers are the hatchet-fishes whose bodies are deeply keeled for anchoring the pectoral muscles. These are the only fishes capable of true flight; they leap out of the water and fly considerable distances over the surface by whirring their pectoral fins – so any tank containing hatchet-fishes must be covered. Two species are common, the Silver *bottom left* and the Marbled *top centre*. Mollies, also surface dwellers, have mouths shaped for capturing mosquito larvae. One orange Molly feeds with a shoal of black Mollies *bottom right*. But beware of another surface feeder, the baby Arawana *top left*. A fingerling may look appealing, but will soon be devouring all the other fishes in the tank. Similarly, young Tinfoil Barbs *top right* are pretty, but their growth rate is prodigious. These are bottom-feeding fishes as their downward-directed mouths indicate, but they readily rise to the surface to take any floating food.

Swivel-eyes

Fishes that live in bright waters rely on sight to find food and detect predators, so have well developed eyes. They have good colour vision, are especially sensitive to movement, but are not so good at making out shapes. The typical fish's eye is circular with a round or pear-shaped pupil. The Spotted Sucking Catfish *top left* has most unusual half-moon shaped pupils. The eyes of most fishes appear to be immobile, staring for ever sideways into space. But fishes' eyes are actually moving most of the time, each eye swivelling independently of the other. This is less easy to see in streamlined fishes whose eyes are set flush with the side of the head, but obvious in the sea-horse whose conning-tower eyes are constantly turning to scan its surroundings. The Porcupine-fish *bottom left* can glance back over its shoulder with one eye while looking forward with the other, and a feeding Discus *right* becomes quite cross-eyed as it focuses stereoscopically for a close-up look at a Tubifex worm before deciding to eat it.

Feelers

Catfishes, like cats, have long-distance feelers for sensing their position by touch. Catfishes are mainly nocturnal or live in dark murky waters where food-finding by sight is impractical. Many have two or three pairs of barbels on upper and lower lip giving them a pro-lifically-whiskered appearance. The Painted Catfish *bottom left* has exception-ally long fine barbels that enable it to identify any object it touches in the dark. The Glass Catfish *top left* has but one pair of barbels. Unlike other catfishes this species is not a bottom-dweller, but hovers obliquely among water plants.

The beautiful silvery-gold barb from Thailand *top right* swims in mid-water but finds much of its food by feeling and smelling along the bottom. It has two pairs of small flexible barbels which work over the mud locating small edibles that might otherwise be missed.

The feelers of the Three-spot Gourami *bottom right* serve the same purpose as barbels but are the ventral fins com-pletely modified into long sensitive organs of touch, taste and smell.

Electric Fishes

There is a small group of fishes, super-ficially dull and uninteresting-looking yet among the most fascinating because they possess a sense which we and most other animals completely lack: the electrical sense.

Several big freshwater species are well known for their ability to generate electricity: the Electric Rays, Electric Stargazer, the Electric Catfish of Africa, and, most powerful of all, the South American Electric Eel. These fishes have been recorded as delivering shocks in excess of 600 volts, which certainly makes them dangerous to man. They use their high-voltage electricity to stun enemies or prey.

There are also over two hundred species of low-voltage electric fishes, including the South American Knife-fish *top left*, the Elephant-trunk Fish of West Africa *centre left*, and the African Knife-fish *bottom left*. Most of these have tiny eyes overgrown by skin, capable only of distinguishing between night and day, but the African Knife-fish has large eyes with a silvery tapetum at the back of the retina *right*, giving it good vision in poor light.

Mildly electric fishes use their elec-tricity to navigate, find food, avoid enemies and communicate with their own kind. They even quarrel by chang-ing frequency to interfere with each other's reception. They only produce between 3 and 10 volts pulsed direct current, but their pulse rate can be enormously high.

Some pulse at only two per second, others at up to 1600 a second. Pulses are produced non-stop by the electric organs which are batteries of converted muscles in the tail. At every impulse the fish's tail becomes momentarily negative, the head positive, turning the fish itself into a kind of bar-magnet producing a spheri-cal field of electric force all around it. Any object nearby distorts the normal pattern of lines of force. Fine pores, corresponding to the taste organs which other fishes have in their skin, react to distortions in the electrical field and send information to a special large elec-trical sense area over the brain.

Most slightly electric fishes live in turbid, swiftly-flowing waters where the usual sense organs would register noth-ing. But the electrical apparatus is so extremely sensitive these fishes can pick up every fine detail of their turbu-lent environment. The slower trans-mitters live in the comparatively quiet backwaters, the fast transmitters in the full spate.

Taste by Touch

The Bronze Armoured Catfish *top left* is a delightful small fish of great character which carries out an important function in the aquarium by going over the bottom like an animated suction cleaner, vacuuming up any food remains that might otherwise lie uneaten.

Larger and more whiskery but also excellent garbage collectors are the naked catfishes. A bewildering array of strange fishes is found in West African rivers and new or rare species are frequently imported into this country. Many have no common name, and have not been scientifically described. The golden-spotted catfish with the beautiful eyes *top and bottom right* is one such nameless naked catfish.

Catfishes are not fussy feeders; they will devour anything edible small enough to be sucked up. They are nocturnal scavengers and though many have large eyes they do not use them to locate food. Instead, they taste their food from a distance, by means of taste-buds on their barbels. As soon as a barbel touches a fragment of food it is seized and eaten. Some catfishes even

have taste-buds all over their bodies and can actually taste with their tails, a great asset when foraging in dark, murky waters.

Catfishes appear to munch their food as if savouring it. A fish's tongue is a flat gristly projection from the floor of the mouth. It has no muscles, so cannot move, but it has taste-buds and can distinguish between flavours. Many fishes are acutely sensitive to sour, salt and bitter tastes, but cannot detect sweetness.

Most fishes have a keen sense of smell. Like ours, their sense receptors are located in the nostrils, but their nostrils are little holes, paired in some species, in the top of the snout. When food is dropped into their tank, fishes become very excited; they can smell it even if they cannot see it. If a fish is hurt, its grazed skin releases a warning substance which other fishes can smell in minute concentrations. Some species react by panic flight, whereas the fear reaction of shoaling species is to bunch together. A loud noise or sudden movement near their tank will also cause fish such as Monos and Scats to bunch together *bottom left*.

17

Yawning

Warm-blooded animals yawn when they wake up and when they are tired. The yawn takes in an extra supply of oxygen and the stretch that goes with the yawn sends the blood flowing faster, carrying the extra oxygen to the muscles, so banishing fatigue.

When a fish such as the Electric-blue Damsel *left* yawns, it too stretches, by spreading fins and gill covers. The purpose of a fish's yawn is to prepare for action. Fishes are most active in the middle of the day, and that is when they yawn most often, when they have been either stationary or only moving about slowly, then see the need for fast action when for instance an enemy or food appears. The Three-spined Stickleback *top right* has been quietly patrolling his nesting territory when suddenly a rival

male intrudes and challenges him. He yawns and stretches his spines and fins, driving the blood faster round his body and giving his muscles more energy for the impending threat display and possible attack on the intruder. The Pike Cichlid *bottom right*, a voracious predator lying in wait among the weeds, has also spotted another fish, in this case potential prey. Yawning, he tones up his muscles before the pounce.

Burton's Mouthbrooder *above* reveals such a big gape when it yawns that were it not for the draw-string muscles closing the gullet we would be able to see right down its throat.

Big Mouths

The South American Leaf-fish is an interesting species but definitely not one for the mixed community tank; it can devour prey measuring up to three-quarters of its own length. It lurks among weeds or stones, superbly camouflaged by its leaf-like shape and colour. When a smaller fish such as a Guppy swims within range the Leaf-fish glides from its hiding place *left*. The Guppy is at one moment swimming unconcernedly and at the next has vanished. Only a few gulping movements and several prodigious yawns reveal that the Leaf-fish has fed *bottom right*.

Archer-fish *top right* are also large-mouthed predators. They take food from underwater or from the surface in the normal way but also have a unique method of shooting down insects crawling on leaves overhanging the water. They use the tongue and the roof of the mouth to form a tube through which they spit water by a powerful contraction of their gill covers. How they estimate distance and take accurate aim from underwater is still a mystery. They can also shoot in the eye any unwary aquarist who lifts the lid of their tank!

Cleaner Shrimps

In contrast to Leaf- and Archer-fishes, the Copper-band Butterfly-fish has a minute mouth. Its snout is scissor-like and the tiny mouth only opens enough to suck almost microscopic worms or shrimps from crannies in the coral.

The Copper-band *below left* looks as if it is yawning. Its mouth is as wide as it will stretch, gill covers are gaping and dorsal fin raised. In fact this fish is displaying to the Cleaner Shrimps on the rock, in a special display inviting them to clean it. If the shrimps accept the invitation they will signal with their white antennae *top left*, then swim onto the Copper-band and go over its body picking off tiny parasites with their delicate pincers *right*, even reaching into the gills or mouth to clean inside.

Cleaner Shrimps are decorative and extremely useful in the marine tank. Unlike many other crustaceans, they are completely peaceful towards their own kind, so several may safely be kept with any non-aggressive fishes.

Cleaner Fishes

Like Cleaner Shrimps, the Cleaner Wrasse *top and bottom left and bottom right* is brightly striped to advertise its trade. Also like the shrimps, the wrasse sets up shop and summons fishes to be cleaned by a special display. Fishes such as the Flame Dwarf Angel-fish *left* signal their desire to be cleaned by giving the open-mouthed display *bottom*. During the cleaning operation the wrasse fans its ventral fins to let its host know where it is *top*. When the host has had enough it flicks its fins, closes its mouth and shakes itself before swimming away.

Several other species of fish act as cleaners when young. The yellow wrasse *bottom right* is a juvenile of the Green Moon Wrasse. (Adults are multi-hued in olive-green and orange with blue-green band and red stripes.) The Brown Surgeon-fish *top right* will clean large fishes; here it is pecking the legs of a Spiny Lobster which it probably takes for part of the coral scenery. Cleaners of any kind are invaluable, helping to keep down skin parasites that are always dangerously present and can multiply lethally in an aquarium.

Anemone-fishes

Associations between different kinds of animals are a constant interest. Sea anemones are dangerous to most small fishes because their tentacles are loaded with stinging cells. A sick Triangular Butterfly-fish, for instance, will be held and paralysed by a big anemone, then slowly drawn into its stomach *top left*. But a family of damsel-like fishes, the clown-fishes, have taken to living among the tentacles of certain large sea anemones. Clown-fishes such as Clark's Clown-fish *bottom left* and the Black-finned Orange Clown-fish *right* exude a mucous substance which protects them by inhibiting the anemone from discharging its stinging cells. If a clown-fish loses its mucus it will fall prey to the anemone, so a sick or damaged clown-fish has to leave. The healthy clown-fish, nestled among the anemone's tentacles, is safe from all enemies, but it is doubtful if the anemone gains any advantage at all from the association.

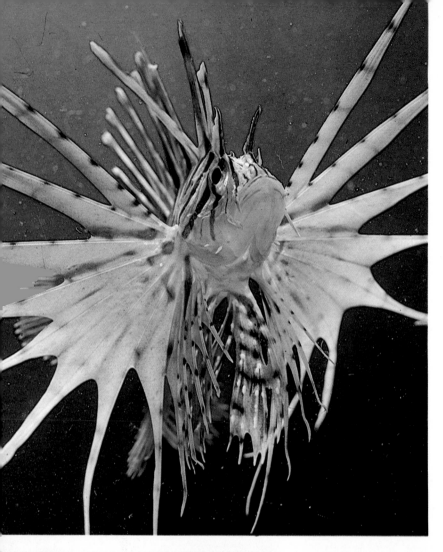

Beware of the Fish

There are some aquarium fishes which must be handled with extra care, not only for their sakes but for the sake of the handler; they are quite capable of inflicting painful, even dangerous, wounds on the unwary aquarist.

The Dragon-fish *top left* is known by many names, all attesting to its offensive nature: Sting-fish, Wasp-fish, Lion-fish, Fire-fish, Scorpion-fish. Its spines contain a poison which can inflict an extremely painful sting, a defence against larger predatory fishes or even aquarists. However, it is only aggressive if provoked; small specimens, calmly handled, make the most amusing aquarium pets. They have enormous mouths and appetites to match, so unfortunately tend to rapidly outgrow their tank.

The Clown Loach *bottom left* is the most brightly coloured of the loaches. Once acclimatised it is hardy, decorative and long-lived. As with many loaches there is a pair of defensive erectile spines in front of the eyes. There is no poison gland, but the knife-like spines easily catch in a net and when trying to extricate the thrashing, entangled fish not only the net but the fish and the handler's fingers may be damaged.

Well-known for its razor-sharp teeth and bloodthirsty nature is the Piranha. It has an unusually big head, for the accommodation of the massive jaw muscles; its jaws are so strong and its teeth so sharp that it can chop out a chunk of flesh as neatly as a surgeon with a scalpel.

In the wild, piranhas hunt in packs and can reduce a large carcase to a skeleton in a matter of minutes. Their ferocity has become legendary but many stories are probably exaggerated. In the aquarium the Red Piranha *right, top and bottom* can be quite timid, but nevertheless will severely damage any hand or catch-net when caught.

The Smooth Trunk-fish *bottom centre* lives among corals. It is slow-moving and unstreamlined. Built like a tortoise, its whole body is encased in a rigid box, only its tail and fins are movable. Although harmless in appearance it can give out a powerful poison. When this happens in an aquarium other fishes show signs of distress and quickly die. Only tough characters are not affected, such as the Caribbean Scorpion-fish, itself well endowed with poison spines.

Puffers

Puffers are peaceful and amusing fishes. Their large forward-looking eyes and rounded faces set off by fluttering ear-like pectoral fins give them a teddy bear look. However, puffers have very serviceable teeth fused into a sharp beak with which they nip up even well-protected food such as barnacles, sea snails, crabs and tube worms, or the unprotected fingers of an inquisitive human. And their affable expression belies the fact that their bodies contain one of the deadliest poisons found in nature. The poison, tetraodontoxin, is an alkaloid very similar to the deadly poison muscarin found in some toadstools; the symptoms from eating pufferfishes and Death Cap fungi are similar. The result of either may prove fatal.

A common marine species of puffer is the Porcupine-fish *top left*. Small specimens are frequently imported and make interesting aquarium inmates. They appear to be phlegmatic creatures. Enclosed in a fairly tough thorny skin, and of a none-too-streamlined shape, they cruise unhurriedly about as if afraid of no-one. Quite apart from their poison which does not benefit the individual since it can only operate after its own death, they, like other puffers, possess another unique defence system: a false stomach or bladder which they can inflate by swallowing water or air in a series of rapid gulps. As an alarmed puffer inflates *centre left*, its spines stand up, so that when fully inflated *bottom left* the fish has turned into a living thorny balloon, almost impossible for most predators to swallow. Newly-imported Porcupine-fish may inflate at the least alarm, such as the tank light being suddenly switched on; but a tame fish is almost impossible to shock into inflating unless handled.

A close relative of the Porcupine-fish is the Horned Balloon-fish *top right*, the surface of whose eyes reflect a beautiful green-blue.

As well as marine puffers there are a few species found in brackish and fresh water. The Green Puffer of Southeast Asia thrives in the brackish water tank with other peaceful species such as the Scat. With its powerful beak the puffer chops up a large shrimp *top centre*. The Scat hovers nearby, ready to dart in and snap up any unconsidered trifles which, with its small soft mouth, it could not have bitten up for itself *bottom right*.

Camouflage

The Batfish *left* lives in coastal waters and mangrove swamps. It strongly resembles a dead mangrove leaf, both in its shape and coloration and also in its manner of swimming when threatened by a predator. To escape notice, it turns on its side and drifts with the current among the floating leaves, or even lies motionless among the dead leaves on the bottom.

A very young Batfish makes an attractive and interesting aquarium pet. It is extremely elegant, with very long dorsal and ventral fins. Once acclimatised it is quite hardy and can grow at a spectacular pace. As it grows, the relative fin-length decreases and the colour bands become less distinct, so that the adult finishes up almost circular in shape and a uniform silver-grey. By this time it has far outgrown the home tank, but makes a splendid exhibit in one of the large public aquaria. In the wild the adults forsake the mangrove shallows and live in deeper water around coral reefs.

Similar to the young Batfish in shape are the freshwater Angels *bottom right;* long-finned, vertically striped, oval fishes which appear to dwindle to wafer-thin creatures when they turn and present themselves head-on. They are slow and stately swimmers, admirably suited to the large well-planted tank, and are long-established favourites with aquarists. Whether sideways on or facing the watcher their camouflage is superb; either their shape or their stripes or both blending with the vertical stems of the plants among which they live – or even with the stripe of a larger Angelfish behind.

Also well known for their superb camouflage are the flatfishes. Occasionally tiny specimens of the South American Freshwater Sole *top right* are imported. In the wild these often swim up estuaries with the tide as does the European Sole and may live for a while in freshwater, but in captivity they do better in brackish water rather than in a purely freshwater tropical tank. Like other kinds of flatfishes they can change their colour to match the background on which they lie. Their flattened shape casts no shadow to draw attention. Only their revolving eyes, set in little turrets above the head and constantly swivelling to watch for danger or food, may betray the fish's position. The eyes of Batfish and Angel are less conspicuous, obscured by camouflaging strips.

Sea-horses

When Golden Sea-horses are imported they are generally almost black *bottom left*. They need to settle down on their own in a well-established tank furnished with living coral rocks, fanworms and other filter-feeding invertebrates, and planted with flourishing *Caulerpa* alga. Sea-horses are fastidious and slow feeders which cannot stand competition from greedy fishes such as damsels. Some sea-horse species will only take live food such as small shrimps, baby Guppies or mosquito larvae, but Golden Sea-horses quickly take to frozen Fairy Shrimps *(Mysis)* which can be bought from pet stores. When settled in and feeding well Golden Sea-horses soon begin to lighten in colour, gradually assuming a speckled dun *right*. After four to six weeks they will have turned a beautiful deep golden yellow *top left*. But if conditions in their tank are not right, they will remain black.

Colour Changes

Fishes' colours change not only according to their state of health but according to the seasons and also to an individual's emotions. Fishes' colours are often a compromise between achieving camouflage as a protection against predators and being conspicuous to a mate or rival. In many species such as the Black Ruby Barb *left* young fishes, females and non-breeding males alike are coloured in a disruptive pattern of light and dark vertical stripes *top* which help a fish remain almost invisible among weed. At the approach of the breeding season the male needs to show himself off to prospective mates and intimidate rival males, so he gradually assumes his nuptial red coloration *centre*. The female remains black-and-gold striped. At the height of the breeding season the Black Ruby male is a deep blood-red *bottom left*, the most beautiful of the many species of small tropical barbs.

In the breeding season male Firemouth Cichlids are resplendent with fiery throats. They are extremely aggressive fish; two males in a tank quarrel relentlessly. The dominant male may chivy his subordinate to death in the end, unless one or other is removed. Well-matched males engage in lip-tugging contests. In this case *top right* the subordinate male had somehow succeeded in dislocating the lips of the other fish during a struggle. With its main weapon of offence out of action the once dominant fish was quite demoralised and assumed the pale submissive colours of a subordinate, while the colours of the winner intensified. A helping human hand caught up the loser, replaced his protruding lips and then housed him in a separate tank where he quickly regained his composure and his fierce colours.

Many other species of fish can pale with fright or intensify their colours at will. If a group of Angelfishes *bottom right* is watched closely the individuals can be seen changing colour as they move around. This in itself can have a camouflaging effect; one moment there is a silvery fish-shaped object, the next it has disappeared, its dark stripes obscuring the fishy outline and blending it with the vertical light and dark patterns of sunlit leaves and their shadows. By the same means these peaceful cichlids may also be signalling to the other members of the shoal.

Displays

In the wild, male fishes fighting for territorial space hardly ever injure one another because their displays are all put on for effect. The weaker fish usually soon acknowledges that discretion is the better part of valour and retires from the scene. Most displays make an individual appear larger, stronger or more ferocious than he actually is. The male Sailfin Molly *left* spreads his huge dorsal fin and angles himself so that his rival is intimidated by his apparently superior size. This male had previously had a section bitten from the front of his dorsal fin, but the fin is regenerating and, though not restored to its full splendour, still functions efficiently as a threat signal.

Among shoaling fishes such as the Scat *top right* the dorsal fin display is used by a small fish when it swims near a larger one. It is as though the smaller fears being bullied on account of its size and so tries to make itself look big. For the same reason the Spanish Hog-fish *bottom right* over-reacts towards the larger Rock Beauty by presenting a fierce open-mouth display.

Swordtails

The Swordtail is ever popular, decorative, colourful and undemanding, and readily produces its many large broods of live young even in the beginner's community tank. The wild coloration is mainly olive green but under domestication a variety of colour forms have evolved, such as the albino *top left* and the red *bottom left*. The Swordtail readily crosses with the Platy and hybrids have given rise to further colour varieties with varying fin lengths. Lyre-tail Swordtails are illustrated *right;* a red female and a male tuxedo.

There is a strong social hierarchy in any Swordtail community, with a peck order related to the size and aggressiveness of individuals. Dominance is decided and maintained by aggressive displays. Swordtail males fight with their swords, although since these are lengthened soft fins they do no injury with them. Sword-flashing males *bottom left* swim rapidly backwards at one another in a fencing display, although actual bullying of subordinates is done by nipping with the mouth. Females also fence with one another even though they lack swords.

Mirror Displays

Many brightly coloured small coral reef fishes are so highly territorial that only one of a given species can be kept in any one tank. In the wild, such fishes maintain home stretches of reef for their own exclusive use by rushing out and attacking any individual of the same or related species, often seeing off fishes far bigger than themselves. In order to witness the displays of these fishes without subjecting them to possible injury, a useful piece of equipment is a small pocket mirror set against a rock in the tank. Aggressive species will give a splendid exhibition as soon as they catch sight of their own reflections.

Marine angel-fishes are most intolerant towards their own kind. Young specimens are often spectacularly colourful and quite different from the adults which are mainly dull unpatterned blackish-grey. The young Rock Beauty *top left* is predominantly orange-yellow, the juvenile French Angel *top right* is black with yellow stripes, and even more striking is the young Koran Angel *bottom left*, with its vivid blue and white stripes. All these angel-fishes attack their own reflections with great vigour, trying to bite them and swimming alongside to shove them or aim tailbeats at them. Equally colourful and aggressive are the tiny Beau Gregories *top right*, but the Sharp-nosed Swellfish, a kind of puffer, was more curious than aggressive *top left*, while the female Bluehead Wrasse *also top left*, a shoaling species, kept looking behind the mirror in an attempt to find the companion that had apparently disappeared there.

Rainbow Cichlids *bottom right* are relatively peaceful for cichlids, but breeding pairs do best with a tank to themselves. This species is unusual in that the female has the brightest colouring. She displays her pink belly by twisting herself into a sort of bulbous S-shape in front of her mirror "rival", while the male displays in a more restrained manner before his own "rival".

Pugilists

The Jack Dempsey *top left and top right* was aptly named after the famous boxer; it is one of the most aggressive cichlids. Rival males at first display laterally at each other with raised fins and intensified colours. If neither is intimidated, they circle one another and finally each grabs the other by the mouth in a trial of strength. Well-matched rivals may engage in mouth-pulling for four hours before one of them concedes the battle.

Three-spined Stickleback males *bottom right* also display sideways at one another with raised spines and throats glowing. When neither gives way they spin round trying to bite. If one fish acknowledges defeat, he is hurried over the territorial boundary by a parting nip from the victor.

The silver Apollo Rasbora is not often kept, although a shoal of fingerlings is quite a pretty sight. Older fishes joust for living room by swimming alongside one another in an open-mouth shoving match *bottom left*. This species of rasbora rapidly outgrows the average tank, and is too lively and restless for community life.

Vibrations

Fighting fishes, such as the Tiger Barbs *right*, may swim alongside one another flailing their tails. This is part of the fight ritual known as tail-beating. The tail-beaters do not strike each other directly, but shoot a wave of water at one another, often with enough force to knock the opponent off balance and send plants swirling.

The use of pressure waves is a further method by which fishes communicate. It supplements and reinforces signals received through the eyes. For instance shoaling fishes each maintain their individual distances from the nearby members of the shoal not only from seeing the other fishes but from feeling their proximity as well.

The majority of fishes are extremely sensitive to changes of pressure in the water, this sensitivity being a function of the lateral line, a canal under the scales which can be seen as a dotted line of small pores curving from gill cover to tail. When strong shock waves hit a fish it is equivalent to us being buffeted by a gale. The Silver Badger-fish *top left* is reacting with spread fins to just such a shock.

The sense of vibration in fishes is so well developed it can even replace the sense of sight. The Blind Cave-fish *bottom left* is totally blind, but its lateral line is well developed so that it can find its way about by detecting minute changes of pressure in the water; these are mostly caused by the tiny waves it sets up as it swims, which then bounce back from objects around it. The Cave-fish is found in underground rivers in limestone caves in Mexico. In the aquarium it manages just as well as sighted fishes.

Besides detecting pressure waves, most fishes can also hear sound waves transmitted through the water. Like other vertebrate animals they have an internal ear. Members of the carp family, to which the Tiger Barb belongs, have a well developed sense of hearing, said to be as good as our own in a few species. Fishes have no vocal chords, but many can produce grunts and squeaks. In addition some fishes are quite noisy feeders, others make a din shovelling gravel, so that the aquarium is often far from the quiet peaceful place we on the outside take it to be.

Headstanders, Tailstanders

The majority of aquarium fishes manage very well swimming in a horizontal position, but several South American characins have slightly odd swimming habits. The Headstander *top left* is found in sluggish weed-choked waters where it glides slowly over the bottom with its head down. In this position it closely resembles a dead leaf, both in shape and colour. It feeds on small plants and invertebrates and its headstanding posture probably allows it to nibble in places other fishes cannot reach. In contrast, the Penguin-fish *top right* normally swims standing on its tail. This is a peaceful, shoaling little species. Its oblique posture and the strong black line down its side makes it quite hard to see among the leaves and stems of water plants.

Headstanding and tailstanding are also used by many otherwise horizontal

fishes as a means of communication. The butterfly-fishes *bottom left* appear to be bowing to one another; in fact bowing in fishes has the same function as it does in human society, serving to acknowledge the superiority of the other person. The Rainbow Butterfly *right* bows more deeply, indicating that its rank is inferior to that of the Golden Butterfly which has angled itself to bite the submissive fish rather than show submission itself. The Angelfish, on the other hand, indicates lower social status by tailstanding *bottom right*. When young Angelfishes are first put together in a tank a certain amount of threat display and pecking goes on in order to establish a social order. Rank-relationships are fought out in pairs, but once the peck order has been established there is little further fighting unless another Angel is introduced. The newcomer's very strangeness reduces his aggression, and he signals this by tailstanding. He automatically takes his place as the lowest in rank, and is obliged to fight his way up from the bottom to better his social position.

Siamese Fighters

Siamese Fighting Fishes owe their name to the extraordinary pugnacity of the males. Wild fishes are highly territorial though not as showy as the domesticated forms, which like fighting cocks and racehorses, have been bred and exploited for public contest for generations. Under domestication numerous long-finned Fighters have been developed in blue, emerald, wine-red, orange, white and black.

Siamese Fighter males are best kept in small individual tanks arranged in a row so that the fishes can see each other. The resulting rivalry leads to continual fin-spreading and the development of fine colours. One male may be kept in the community tank but he will not exhibit his splendour in isolation from his own kind. If two Siamese Fighter males are put together they will immediately begin their war dance, swimming parallel to one another with fins billowing and gill covers spread. Suddenly they lunge at one another, biting, rasping scales from flanks, tearing magnificent finnage to shreds. Well-matched rivals may continue fighting for hours. However, frequent pauses in the battle have to occur for breathing; both fishes, usually together, rise to the surface for a gulp of fresh air *left*. Siamese Fighters are Labyrinth fishes; they have a lung-like respiratory organ, the labyrinth, which enables them to breath air. Their gill respiration has been so reduced that if they are prevented from reaching the surface to breath they drown.

The Siamese Fighter male builds a nest of air bubbles among floating plants *top right*. Each bubble is mouthed and coated with a tough slime so that a foam raft is formed for the safe keeping of eggs and fry.

A courting Siamese Fighter can be just as vicious towards a female as he is to another male; if the female is not ready to spawn he may bite her to death. The courtship display *bottom right* looks similar to the aggressive display. If the female is ripe she allows herself to be driven beneath the bubble nest. Here she turns on her back and, with the male wrapped around her, lays her eggs into the nest. Any that fall are retrieved by the male and spat among the bubbles. The male guards the eggs and the young fry for several days after they hatch. After spawning, the female must be removed or the male will kill her.

Kissing Gouramis

Another member of the Labyrinth family is the Kissing Gourami, so named because two fishes will often "kiss" *bottom left*. Both adults and young kiss each other. They also mouth stones, submerged branches, leaves of water plants and so on, which makes interpretation of kissing difficult. It is thought that kissing may be a form of communication or threat display, since fishes will kiss each other's flanks *top left*, sometimes spinning around mouthing each other's tails *right* as if trying to bite rather than showing affection. When kissing inanimate objects they are presumably feeding by scraping off algae or picking up fine food particles.

Like fighting Siamese Fighters that need to pause in the battle in order to take a breath, kissing Kissing Gouramis have to surface for air every few minutes or they would suffocate. Only young fishes are suitable for the home aquarium, since a full grown adult would span a dinner plate–in fact in its native South-east Asia this species is a highly esteemed food fish.

Courtship

The Rasboras are mostly small peaceful fishes which occur in great shoals in rivers and lakes throughout South-east Asia. Some are exceptionally hard to breed, others not difficult if given the right conditions: shallow water, soft and acid, at a fairly high temperature. The courting Clown Rasbora male dances around the female *top left* with back arched and dorsal fin erect. Their eggs stick to the leaves of water plants and hatch in about twenty-four hours.

The Golden Sailfin Molly *bottom left*, an estuarine species, does best in the aquarium in hard alkaline water to which sea salt has been added. Courtship can often be observed: the male speads his magnificent dorsal sail in display, and also stimulates the female by butting her flank. Mollies are live-bearing tooth-carps; the eggs develop within the female after internal fertilization by the male who has a gonopodium, the trans-formed anal fin, for the introduction of the sperm. It is very rare to see the mating of livebearers, but most species repro-duce readily in densely planted tanks. One mating can fertilise several broods.

From Lake Malawi in central Africa

come many species of colourful cichlids.
(In this lake there are over two hundred
not found anywhere else in the world.)
The Golden Cichlid *top right* is one of the
most beautiful. The female and all ju-
veniles are golden with three distinct
black longitudinal bands. The male in
breeding livery has exactly the same
pattern, but the ground colour is black
with brilliant blue bands. Only the
dominant males in a shoal are black,
subordinate males are golden. If
alarmed, a male rapidly loses his brilliant colour and becomes female-hued.
This male is coming into breeding con-
dition but has not yet replaced his
golden banding with blue.

Several other species of Lake Malawi
cichlids have blue-black males and
golden females. Sometimes a "pair"
turns out to be a male of one species and
a female of another *bottom left*. This male
John James' Cichlid courted the female
Bigeyes Cichlid, dancing before her and
trying to lead her to a spawning stone
by displaying the egg-spots in his anal
fin. But her only response was to fly at
him aggressively. In the wild, hybrid-
ization between similar species is
prevented by geographical or beha-
vioural barriers. In the aquarium, cross-
breeding could occur.

Spawning

The Swordtail, like the Sailfin Molly, is a livebearing tooth-carp. Pregnant females can be recognised by the pregnancy mark, a black spot on the belly. A female about to give birth hovers in a characteristic manner. At the moment of birth *top left* the egg membrane is usually ruptured. The baby is ejected and the female simultaneously jerks away *bottom left*. Almost immediately, the tiny Swordtail swims up to the surface to fill its swim bladder with air, then begins to feed. From the moment of birth the baby is independent of its mother, who takes no interest in her brood except as a potential meal.

Angelfish *right* spawn on the broad leaf of a water plant which they first clean by pecking off all sediment and algae. The female glides over the leaf depositing her eggs over which the male then follows discharging milt. Both parents care for the clutch, continually fanning fresh water over the eggs with their pectoral fins. When the young are ready to hatch, they are chewed out of the egg-shells by the parents and spat onto leaves where they hang by short threads. In another day or so the fry are transferred to small nursery pits. Then, when about a week old, the whole brood follows the parents out to find food.

Mouthbrooding

Most effective of all forms of parental care in fishes is that known as mouthbrooding; after spawning one of the parents picks up the newly-laid eggs and carries them around in the mouth until they hatch. The fry are released for short periods as they grow, but return to the parent's mouth for protection if danger threatens. In some species the male carries the eggs, in others the female. Either way, mouthbrooding gives eggs and young maximum protection from being eaten by other fishes.

Many African cichlids are mouthbrooders. The high degree of protection given to their broods is correlated with the very high density of fishes in Africa's lakes. Burton's Mouthbrooder *top left* is a species in which the female is the brooder. The male has a row of conspicuous spots on his anal fin; the female has fewer, less well-marked, spots. One theory about these spots is that, like many other patterns in fishes, they are simple recognition marks, enabling males and females of the same species to identify one another.

However, there is a second, very attractive, theory. At spawning, the female Burton's Mouthbrooder turns and snaps up her eggs *centre left* so quickly that the male has no time to shed milt over them. But the male's anal fin spots mimic her new-laid eggs, and he displays these spots on the spawning stone, draping them before the female. In going to collect what she takes to be more eggs *bottom left* the female sucks in sperm, thus ensuring that the eggs are fertilized in her mouth. The drawback to this elegant theory is that some other species of African mouthbrooders which lack egg-dummies apparently manage fertilization in precisely the same manner.

When spawning is complete, the female's throat is bulging with eggs *top right*. Usually she fasts throughout the brooding period. When the young hatch they remain in the mother's mouth until the yolks are absorbed. After ten to fifteen days from fertilization they are released – the mother simply opens her mouth and they swim out. However, if danger threatens, the mother calls her young to her using posture and colour signals. The babies crowd around her mouth and she gulps them in in batches. When the danger has passed she spits them all out again *bottom right*.

Paternal Care

In a few species the father alone looks after the brood. The male Three-spined Stickleback prepares a nest for the eggs, collecting a heap of fine plant material, poking it into place and tamping it down with his snout *top left*. Then he swims slowly over it spraying it with a secretion from his kidneys to cement the material together *bottom left*. By diving through the heap he converts the nest into a tunnel tent. A gravid female is lured to the nest by a special dance, the male zig-zagging in front of her displaying his fiery throat. At the nest he points out the entrance *top centre* and, when she goes inside, he nudges her flanks to stimulate spawning, then follows her through the tunnel depositing sperm over the eggs. Several females may be induced to spawn in the same nest, which the male guards with an S-bend ownership display *top right* while the eggs are developing. After the fry hatch he guards the babies *bottom right* until they are big enough to go their own ways.

Family Life

Jewel-fish are among the most beautiful of all cichlids, and, with their exemplary family life, among the most rewarding to watch. But like the majority of cichlids, they are extremely aggressive and each pair must have a tank to themselves. Like Angelfish and some other cichlids Jewel-fish parents share in the care of their brood. They choose a large flat stone on which to spawn, and pick it clean of detritus and algae. The female spawns while moving in a circle or spiral, the male swimming round and milting where she has just laid *top left*. Together they guard the eggs, taking it in turns to fan fresh water over them. When the fry hatch, the parents gather them up in their mouths and transfer them to a nursery on another specially cleaned stone. If any young stray while learning to swim, they are retrieved and spat back into the nursery *bottom left*. When free-swimming, the young stay with the parents in a small shoal *right*, a delightful family group.

INDEX

First published in Great Britain 1978 by Colour Library International Ltd.,
Designed by David Gibbon. Produced by Ted Smart.
© Text: Jane Burton © Illustrations: Bruce Coleman Ltd.
Colour separations by La Cromolito, Milan, Italy.
Display and Text filmsetting by Focus Photoset, London, England.
Printed and bound by L.E.G.O. Vicenza, Italy.
Published by Crescent Books, a division of Crown Publishers Inc.
All rights reserved.
Library of Congress Catalogue Card No. 77-18621

CRESCENT 1978